BLAST OFF!
COMETS
AND ASTEROIDS

Helen and David Orme

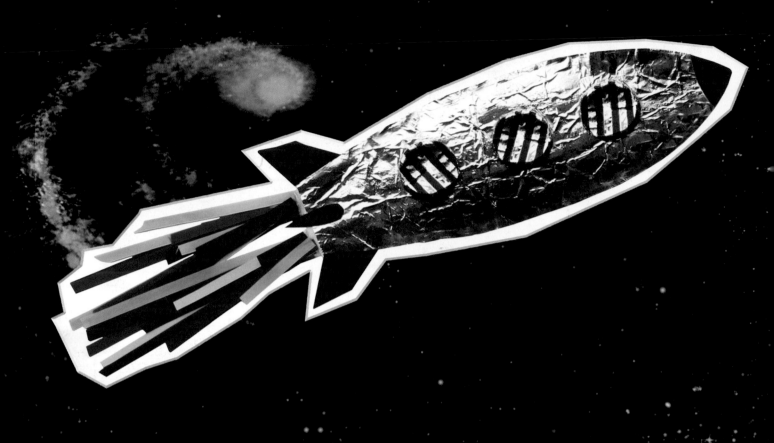

Copyright © ticktock Entertainment Ltd 2007

First published in Great Britain in 2006 by ticktock Media Ltd.,
Unit 2, Orchard Business Centre, North Farm Road,
Tunbridge Wells, Kent, TN2 3XF

ticktock project editor: Julia Adams
ticktock project designer: Emma Randall

We would like to thank: Sandra Voss, Tim Bones, James Powell,
Indexing Specialists (UK) Ltd.

ISBN 978 1 84696 057 4
Printed in China
A CIP catalogue record for this book is available from the British Library.

Picture credits
t=top, b=bottom, c=centre, l-left, r=right, bg=background
Brigdeman: 17b; Corbis: 20; NASA: 7tr, 7cl, 7c, 7bl, 10, 11, 16, 22, 23t; Science Photo Libary: 4/5bg (original), 8, 14, 15t;
Shutterstock: 2/3bg, 6, 7cr, 9t, 24bg; ticktock image library: front cover, 1 all, 5tr, 6/7bg, 9b, 10/11bg, 12, 13, 14/15bg, 15br,
15bl, 17t, 18/19bg, 18, 19, 21, 22/23bg, 23;
Every effort has been made to trace the copyright holders, and we apologise in advance for any unintentional omissions.
We would be pleased to insert the appropriate acknowledgements in any subsequent edition of this publication.

Contents

The Solar System

The **solar system** is made up of the Sun, the planets and moons, and many thousands of smaller objects. These objects are called comets and asteroids.

Sun

Mercury

Venus

Earth

Mars

Jupiter

Asteroid Belt

The solar system was formed millions of years ago from a spinning disc of gas and dust. Most of the material formed the Sun.

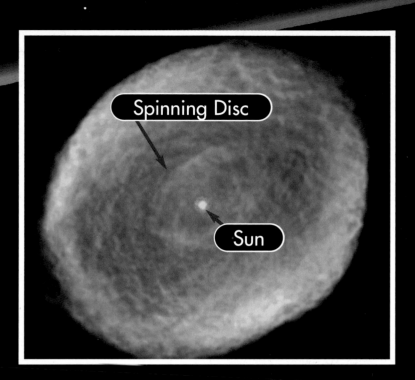

Spinning Disc

Sun

Some material made the planets and the Moon. The rest of the material made the comets and asteroids.

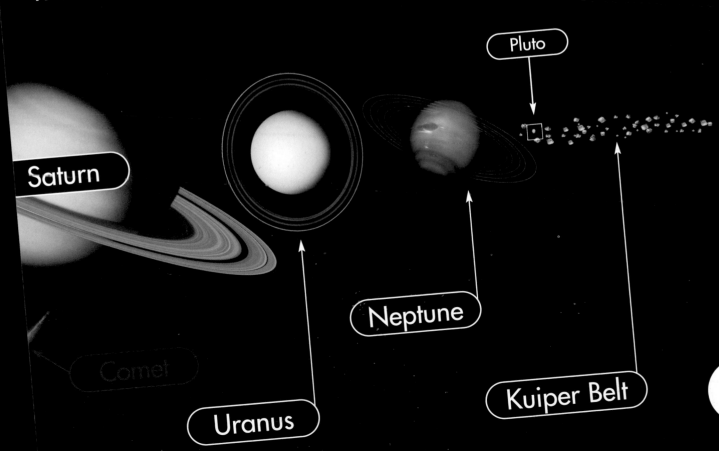

Pluto

Saturn

Neptune

Comet

Kuiper Belt

Uranus

What is an Asteroid?

An asteroid is a rocky object, like a small planet. Most asteroids are less than 2 kilometres across, but some are much bigger.

asteroids

This is Ceres. It is the biggest asteroid that has been discovered up until now. It is nearly 1000 km across.

Ceres

This picture shows how big Ceres is compared to our Moon and the Earth. Because of its size, **astronomers** now call Ceres a **dwarf planet**.

Ceres (998 km)

3476 km

Moon

12,756 kilometres

Earth

Most asteroids are not round like Ceres. This is also a picture of an asteroid, but it is a very bumpy one.

Where are Asteroids?

The first asteroids were discovered in the Asteroid Belt. This is a part of the **solar system**. It is between the **orbits** of Mars and Jupiter and it also orbits the Sun.

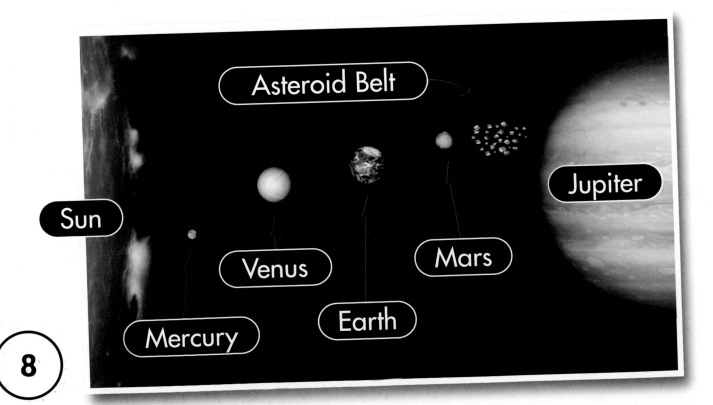

Asteroid Belt

Sun

Jupiter

Venus

Mars

Earth

Mercury

shooting star

Some asteroids are not very far away from Earth. Very tiny ones often reach the Earth. They usually burn up in the **atmosphere**. We call these **shooting stars** or meteors.

Some meteors manage to reach the ground. They are then called **meteorites**. This is a picture of a meteorite that was found in Los Angeles in the USA in October 1999.

1.5 inches

Glossary

Astronomers People who study space, often using a telescope.

Atmosphere The gases that surround a star, planet or moon.

Bayeux tapestry An embroidered wall-hanging. It is about 70 metres long and shows the Norman (French) conquest of England in 1066.

Crater A hole in the surface of a planet or a moon. It is usually made when a rock from space crashes into the surface and leaves a deep dent.

Dwarf planet An object smaller than a planet that orbits around the Sun.

Great Plague A deadly disease. In the 17th century, many people in Europe died from this illness.

Meteorites Pieces of rock that travel through space at high speed and crash into planets or moons.

Orbits The paths that planets or other objects take around the Sun, or satellites take around a planet.

Shooting stars Pieces of rock from space that burn up in Earth's atmosphere. Scientists also call them meteors.

Solar system The Sun and everything that is in orbit around it.

Space probe A spacecraft sent from Earth to explore the solar system. It can collect samples and take pictures.

Index